— Left —

Bronze harness plaque from the 5th century BC, from a chariot grave in France, showing the geometric flourish and metalworking skills of the early Celts.

— Below —

Small terracotta figure of a Celtic warrior from Egypt, 3rd century BC. A detachment of Celtic mercenaries served in the Egyptian army.

Contents

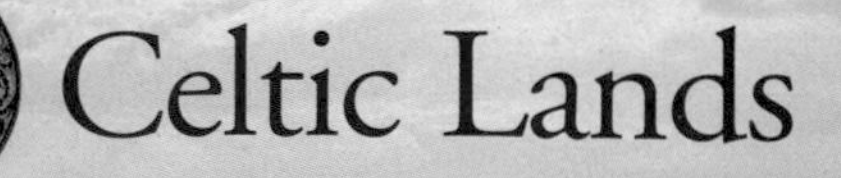

2 Celtic Lands

— Above —

The site of La Tène, on Lake Neuchâtel in Switzerland, where offerings are thought to have been thrown into the water from a wooden jetty.

As Julius Caesar's Roman legions sailed to Britain in 55 BC, warpainted warriors watched from its clifftops, ready for battle with the invaders. These men were Celts, whose tribal brothers in Europe had been fighting Romans for centuries.

An ancient people, the Celts were rooted in central European history beyond 1200 BC. Spreading across the continent, they had split into different tribal groups, sharing an inheritance of language, customs and culture. Around 500 BC the Greeks knew them as 'Keltoi'. To the Romans they were 'Galli' (Gauls), barbarians who swarmed down through the Alpine passes around 400 BC and then sacked Rome. The 'Galatae' invaders of Macedonia and Greece (279 BC) were also Celts. Settling in a region later called Galatia, now part of Turkey, they were defeated a century later by the Romans.

In the 19th century, remains of early Celts were dug up at Hallstatt in Austria. Weapons, brooches, pins, pottery and bronze items were found in the graves of iron-using Celts who had worked the local salt mines in the 7th and 6th centuries BC. More finds, at La Tène on Lake Neuchâtel in Switzerland, uncovered a second stage of Celtic history. Here, north of the Hallstatt area, a new cultural identity was forged in the 5th century BC.

— Above —

A pony cap from Torrs, Scotland, used to protect the animal's head when racing. The style is typically British, from the 3rd or 2nd century BC. The drinking horns were not originally part of it.

— Above —

This bronze axe-head from a cremation grave at Hallstatt, Austria, illustrates the twin Celtic skills of metalworking and horsemanship.

Developing patterns from Mediterranean wine jars, La Tène people produced their own abstract decoration of curling lines, and so created the characteristically 'Celtic' art style.

A taste for Mediterranean wine drew Celtic tribes westward to the Greek colony set up at Massalia (Marseilles) around 600 BC. For wine and other luxuries, they traded gold, tin, amber, fur and slaves. By the 6th century BC, Celts were living across Europe, from Spain to the upper Danube. Miners, metalsmiths, farmers and warriors who built defended hill forts, they were predominant in west and central Europe but were crushed by Roman armies in 225 BC at Telamon in Tuscany.

By 58 BC, when Julius Caesar began his campaigns against them, what remained of the 'free' Celts were centred on Gaul. Reporting on its stubborn Belgae tribes, Caesar mentions their settlements in south-east Britain. This is the only written evidence we have for Celtic migration to the British Isles, although archaeology tells us that Celts had been living here for centuries.

— Above —

A pot from Celtic Britain, made between the 3rd century BC and the Roman conquest. Decorated with strong, simple swirls, it may have been used for storing food or grain and is characteristic of pottery from Maiden Castle, Dorset.

— Above —

A slender iron sword and sheath from La Tène. The weapon was skilfully hammered into a fine cutting blade by an early Celtic smith.

— Above —

North Italian wine flagons inspired the Celtic La Tène art style. This bronze jug from Moselle, France, inlaid with coral and red glass, is based on an Etruscan vessel. Stylized dogs on top chase a duck that 'swims' as the wine pours.

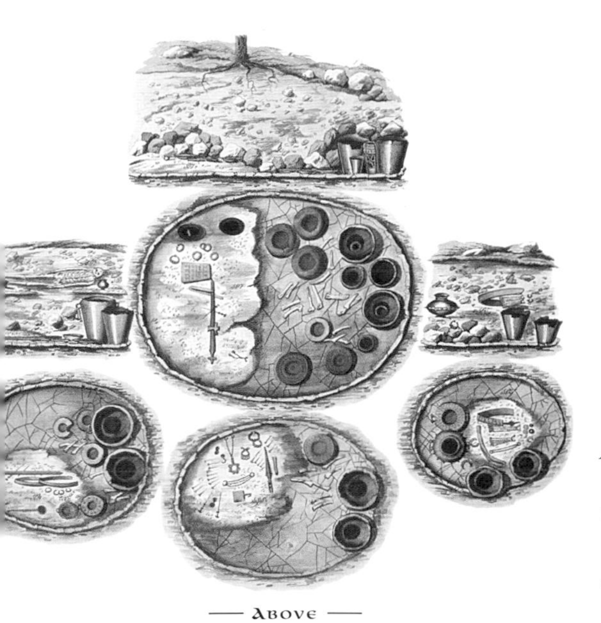

— Above —

Celtic graves and their contents, excavated at Hallstatt (1846–63) by Johann Georg Ramsauer, were carefully recorded in watercolour drawings by Isidor Engel.

4

Celtic Society

The 'civilized' Romans feared the 'barbarian' Celts, although fascinated by their strange customs, savage energy and tactical skill in battle. Bravery, pride, hospitality, boastfulness, unpredictability and a readiness to take offence were other Celtic attributes. They were also renowned drinkers.

Celts lived in family groups, or clans, as part of wider tribal associations that were constantly shifting alliances. A king or chief, with a powerful tribal council of nobles, led a society in which family and community – rather than territory – held the key to a people's identity. Some Celts used 'clientship', or patronage, to reinforce social position, obliging dependants to serve a noble in return for protection, or for work in the case of a craftsman. Clients might belong to other tribes, or whole tribes could become clients of other communities.

Ordinary Celts farmed cattle and crops, while society's top places were won by success in war. Victory brought followers to whom Celtic lords, famed for hospitality and public generosity, distributed gifts to reinforce their prestige. At the base of society were slaves, whose worth might equal a container of wine to be distributed at the tribal feast.

— Above —

Clean, fastidious and proud of their appearance, the Celts produced highly polished, decorated bronze mirrors such as this 1st-century AD example from Desborough, Northamptonshire. Its swirling art style was developed in Britain during the last two centuries BC.

— Above —

Hairdressing a goddess, pictured on the Gundestrup cauldron from Denmark. Celts were reputedly vain; their long, flowing hair was remarked upon by classical authors.

— Above —

A silver-gilt brooch, inset with amber and glass. The Picts who made and wore it in the late 8th century AD were continuing a centuries-old tradition of Celtic decorative metalwork.

— Above —

A rich games-player of the 1st century BC was buried with pieces from his favourite pastime. The glass counters formed sets of four colours, as in the modern game of ludo.

The feast, often wild and drunken, confirmed tribal relationships as men sat in a circle, ranked in order around the most important person – in wealth, birth or battle honour. Status might then be tested. For example, the 'hero's portion' of meat belonged to the bravest warrior, but should a rival rise to claim it, a fight to the death ensured the best man won. In this way, tribal hierarchy was decided.

Tribal identity was maintained by priests who guarded law, learning and custom. Craftsmen were also highly ranked, for they produced the tools, weapons and decorated metalwork that constituted much of the tribe's wealth.

Men occupied the highest levels of society, yet noblewomen may have had more influence than their counterparts in Greece and Rome. Caesar noted that husbands and wives in Gaul pooled equal amounts of money and at death the survivor inherited all. He also remarked that in Britain some women had several husbands. Children may often have been placed with foster parents. 'They do not allow their sons to approach them in public,' commented Caesar, 'unless they have grown up to the age of military service, and they think it a disgrace for a boy under this age to sit in public within sight of his father.'

— Above —

A bronze-crowned skull from Deal, Kent, c.200–100 BC. Buried with sword and shield, the body may have been that of a warrior, although the crown, replicated here, might also signify a chief or priest.

An iron slave chain from Wales, found with a hoard of metal objects in a peat bog, possibly part of a religious offering. The Celts carried iron-working across Europe.

— Above —

This marble copy of a 2nd-century BC bronze of the famous 'Dying Gaul' – actually a Galatian from Turkey – is in the Capitoline Museum, Rome. The figure, naked in battle, wearing a torc around the neck, with spiky lime-washed hair and a drooping moustache, characterizes the Celtic warrior.

Homes and Farms

Quick to absorb new skills, Celts adjusted their farming and building techniques to suit the lands they settled. In Gaul they planted vines to make their own wine. They also grew olives. In Britain, they dragged ploughs twice, crosswise, over small, squarish fields (around 120 x 80m/394 x 262ft). They grew cereals – wheat, barley, oats and rye – with peas, beans, lentils and vetch, and flax for linen. They also coppiced timber for building, fencing and fuel. For food, milk and leather they kept cattle, pigs and small, goat-like sheep, whose coarse wool they wove into weatherproof clothes and cloaks of bright colours and patterns.

Small, hardy cattle were bred for heavy pulling. Horses, much prized, were for warfare, racing and light farm work. The Celtic relish for horse-trading, and the quality of their decorative horse-gear, indicates a high regard for the animal. Dogs were bred for hunting and for their pelts. Chickens from Asia appeared on early Celtic farms.

— Above —
A two-handled bronze kettle used by Hallstatt Celts.

Around 100 BC, farmers cleared more woodland in Britain, drained heavy clay soils, raised bigger cattle herds, improved ploughs and perhaps began rotating crops. A Roman view of Britain's Celtic countryside would still, in places, be familiar – woods, meadows, and fields within ditches, walls or hedges. Traces of Celtic fields, cattle folds, droveways, ditches and settlement enclosures linger over the chalk downland of southern Britain.

In Gaul, Caesar found buildings often 'surrounded by forest … for to avoid the heat they generally seek the neighbourhood of woods and rivers'. In Britain, heat was less of a problem. Here, farming families, together with workers, dependants and animals, lived inside a farmyard area protected

— Left —
This stylized horned head adorns a wrought-iron firedog of the 1st century BC from Welwyn, Hertfordshire. The hearth fire was the focal point of a Celtic home.

Inside an early Iron-Age house, recreated from post holes left by timber supports at Pimperne, Dorset. Bigger than most British buildings of the period, it was probably the home of a noble or chief and so acted as a meeting or feast hall. Celtic houses had one large room, possibly divided, with a hard-packed earthen floor and a framework of tree-trunk poles. The largest houses were 15m (49ft) in diameter, with a 15-tonne straw thatched roof.

Some waterside settlers built artificial island platforms called crannogs, recreated here on Scotland's Loch Tay. Now submerged, they reveal much about everyday Celtic life, as do other waterside settlements such as Glastonbury lake village.

by a bank and ditch. Settlements varied from one home to several, sometimes clustered in unwalled villages, to huge defended hill forts that were more like towns. There were also specialized sites such as those for religious gatherings; a few industrial areas, such as salt works in coastal East Anglia; or trading centres such as Hengistbury Head in Dorset.

While Gauls preferred rectangular buildings, Celtic Britons favoured round houses with conical, sloping roofs thatched by reeds, straw or heather. Walls were usually made of woven twigs (wattle), cemented and weatherproofed with clay daub, although sometimes stones or upright wooden planks were used. There was a doorway but no windows. Animal hides supplied some warmth and comfort, as did the central hearth where a fire of peat or logs cooked the family stew in a heavy iron cauldron suspended above it.

— Above —

Celts made wooden buckets and bowls, but for special occasions produced 'best' vessels decorated with thin sheets of embossed bronze. This bucket from Aylesford, Kent, was used in the 1st century BC, perhaps for diluting wine at tribal feasts.

Art and Language

A Greek of Caesar's time, describing a Celtic tribal feast, recorded that 'among them are also to be found lyric poets whom they call bards. These men sing to the accompaniment of instruments which are like lyres, and their songs may be either of praise or of obloquy.' The Celts accorded high honour to their bards, weavers of words and music. No bardic poetry was written down but, locked in folk memory, echoes of the ancient songs passed down into the legends of Ireland and Wales.

Nor were there any ancient writings to confirm that people in Britain and Ireland were 'Celts', but living languages tell us they were. Two forms of Celtic are spoken to this day in the British Isles – one comprises Irish, Scots and Manx Gaelic, the other Welsh and Cornish.

The Celts also left a trail of place names in Britain, for natural features such as hills and rivers (Thames, Avon and Trent) and through modern counties incorporating old tribal names, such as Devon (the Dumnonii) or Cornwall (the Cornovii). Kent is Celtic, as is Elmet in Yorkshire, a British tribal territory until the 7th century AD. Celtic names abound in Wales and Cornwall. The more hilly and wooded the landscape, the more likely are Celtic place names to be found.

— Above —

Spectacular Iron-Age metalwork from the River Thames includes a 2nd- or 1st-century BC shield boss from Wandsworth, on which bird wings loop in curling tendrils.

From at least 300 BC, Celtic craftsmen in Britain had been creating mirrors, weapons, horse harnesses and torcs in the La Tène art style. And it was in Britain alone – in Wales, Scotland and Ireland – that the style survived the Roman Conquest. Celts loved geometric forms, using iron compasses to create decorative circles, spirals, whorls and ellipses in interlaced patterns filled with engraved lines or dots. They traced twirly plant tendril motifs, adding stylized human or animal faces, often of geese and hares, which they thought magical. Other motifs are familiar today, such as the three-legged triskele, emblem of the Isle of Man.

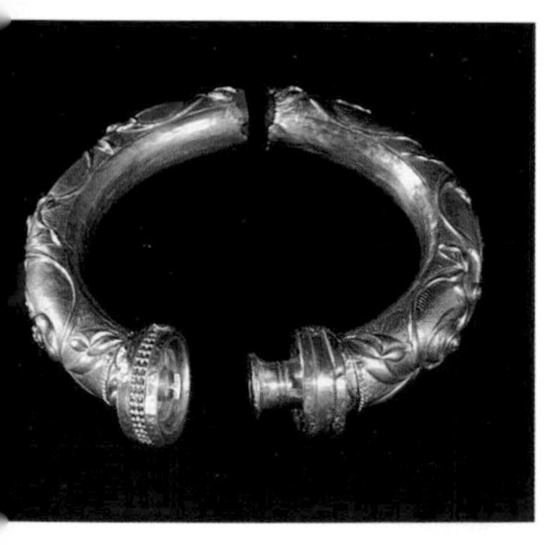

— Above —

A tubular gold torc from a hoard found at Broighter, near Lough Foyle in Ireland. Made locally, probably in the 1st century BC, it displays the high quality of La Tène decorated craftwork in Britain and Ireland.

— Above —

Model boat of gold, from Ireland, with oars and sail. Celtic boats were usually wooden, but coracles were also used. Round and light, with a leather-covered wickerwork frame, coracles were paddled with a single oar, and survived until modern times in west Wales.

Smiths, revered among the early Celts, carried the Iron Age across Europe. They forged iron smelted with charcoal, heating and

— Above —

A variety of Iron-Age horse harnesses illustrates both the intricacies of design produced by Celtic craftsmen and the value placed on their horses by the Celtic people.

— Above —

The 'Petrie Crown', part of a bronze headdress found in Ireland and named after its collector. An elegant example of later La Tène decoration from the British Isles, it dates from the 1st–2nd centuries AD.

hammering it to create strong, flexible swords and farm tools. Bronze and goldsmiths also made smaller decorative items, for Celts loved any adornment, wearing glass beads and bangles in their favourite blues, yellows, reds, greens and white.

Other craftsmen included woodworkers, making anything from bowls to wagons and boats, and potters, who in Britain worked without a wheel almost until Roman times.

— Above —

Celtic battles resounded to the harsh cries of war trumpets (carnyxes). This mouth roundel from an Irish bronze trumpet is probably from the 1st century BC.

Religion and Gods

Ritual and magic linked the Celts to their gods. These spirits of nature demanded rites at shrines and holy places, often in wooded groves or beside water, but also in religious enclosures or temples. Ritual was guarded by Druids, the tribal priests whose name is related to 'oak'. Pliny describes how 'they bring thither two white bulls … Clad in a white robe, the priest ascends the [oak] tree and cuts the mistletoe with a golden sickle ... They then kill the victims ...'. Other forms of human sacrifice, say classical writers, involved 'figures of immense size, whose limbs, woven out of twigs, they fill with living men and set on fire'.

Focal to religious rites were trees and water sources that received offerings to the sacred spirit of the place. The Roman Lucan, writing of rotting wooden idols and branches smeared with human blood, observed that sacrificial death had to fit a god's particular demands. The god Taranis, for example, required burning, and Teutates drowning, while Esus' victims were hanged.

— Above —

Epona, the Celtic horse goddess, on a terracotta relief from France. Popular in Britain and Gaul, the cult of this patroness of mares and foals, of cavalry and travellers on horseback, seems to have spanned the entire Celtic world.

— Above —

A human sacrifice, shown on the Gundestrup cauldron. The victim is either being ritually drowned in a filled container, or about to be pitched down a deep pit-shaft, perhaps to communicate with the underworld.

— Above —

Chariot-burial at Gorton-on-the-Wolds, Yorkshire. Hundreds of Celtic burials, mainly 3rd–1st centuries BC, *were made in this area. Most lay within a square ditch, from which earth was heaped up into a barrow or tumulus over the grave. Some contain wagons or chariots; others had spears hurled into them; one yielded an early coat of mail.*

Other deities, known from inscriptions, include Sul, goddess of the hot spring at Bath, Epona, the horse goddess, and the water goddess, Elen. Dedications to Maponus are found around Hadrian's Wall and to Nodens in Gloucestershire. Some gods were linked in triads; others were shape-shifters, transforming into animals.

The extraordinary 'Lindow Man', a 2,000-year-old victim of Celtic sacrifice, was found preserved in a dried-up bog near Manchester in 1984. This young Celt had been struck unconscious, ritually strangled, stabbed in the throat and then flung face down into a boggy pool. His stomach contained traces of mistletoe, which he may have been given to drink before the sacrifice.

There was a belief in life beyond death, after which, so the Druids taught, the soul passed to another body. Celts were often buried with jewellery, clothes or food, perhaps for the afterlife or in a display of disposable wealth. Ashes buried after cremation might be accompanied with fine metalwork, such as iron firedogs, pottery and Roman wine vessels. The change to cremation, introduced in the last decades BC, reflects a connection with Gaul, where it was already practised.

Celts celebrated four great seasonal festivals, starting with Samain at the end of October, on a night when magic burst loose into the world. This was the turn of the year, when farm animals were slaughtered before winter. Imbolc heralded lambing, in February, and Beltane in May saw the cattle sent out to graze, passing between lighted fires. Lugnasad fell on the first of August, as crops ripened.

In late Roman times came Christianity, which survived in Britain thanks to Celtic monks and missionaries. The native church retained its own style, traditions, saints and stories, rooted in the ancient spirituality of the Celtic world.

— Above —

Roman amphorae for holding wine or fish sauce, together with pots, gaming pieces, food and metalwork, stand in a reconstructed Celtic chief's tomb, ready for use in the afterlife.

— Below —

Celtic crosses, set up at sacred sites, combine traditional Celtic motifs with Christian emblems. They are products of the faith handed down by Christians in Roman Britain via their successors, the Celtic missionary monks who converted the pagan peoples of the British Isles.

12 Celts in Britain

'Land of mist and mystery' was how Britain appeared to the Mediterranean. Yet the isles had been home to Celts since at least the 6th century BC and were known to travellers and traders seeking tin. In the 1st century BC, the Greek Diodorus Siculus reported: 'The inhabitants of Britain ... are especially hospitable to strangers ... they work tin into pieces the size of knucklebones ... the merchants purchase the tin ... and carry it across the Strait to Gaul.'

Defended hill forts, such as Maiden Castle in Dorset, were great tribal centres, which also acted as lookout posts, refuges and markets in Britain from the 6th century BC to the Roman conquest. Spaced across the landscape, mainly from the south coast to north Wales, they dominated their surroundings.

First recorded around 600 BC as Ierne (Ireland) and Albion (Britain), a voyager of 325 BC called the islands 'Pretanic', which mutated to the Roman 'Britannia'. By the 3rd century BC, La Tène people were farming in Britain and 200 years later came the continental Belgae. Settling in the south east, they later led resistance to the Romans they had already fought in Gaul.

Britain's ancient defensive network of hill forts played a part in the operations. Enclosed by banks and ditches, these provided places of safety at times of inter-tribal warfare. Some, like Danebury in Hampshire and Maiden Castle in Dorset, were settlements in which people lived, worked, traded, stored produce and kept their animals. The largest acted as tribal centres.

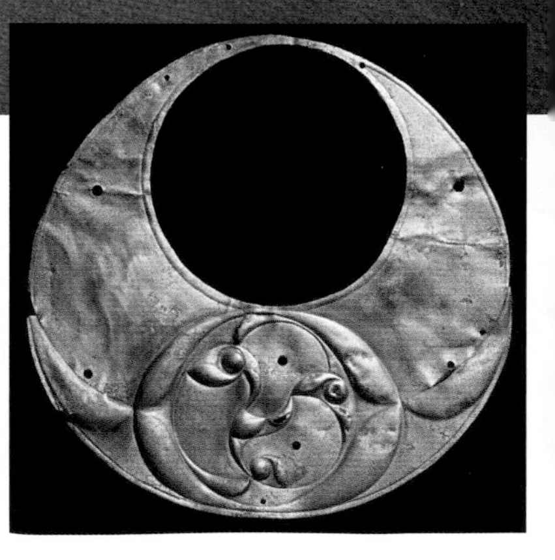

— Above —

Among fine metalwork from the lake deposit at Llyn Cerrig Bach, Anglesey, is a bronze plaque, worn as an ornament, or fastened to a chieftain's chariot.

Other settlements were oppida (towns), the name by which Caesar described sites in Gaul that were larger than villages (vic) and farmsteads. Such centres of regional authority as Camulodunum (Colchester) were often – but not always – tribal capitals. Oppida grew in number as Celtic society became more centralized, with fewer, stronger tribes.

Although some Celts in Britain had joined the fight against Caesar in Gaul, after the first Roman landings in Britain (55 and 54 BC) its people retained links with their Romanized Gaulish neighbours. Caesar's peace treaties underlined the power held by two large blocs in the south east: the Catuvellauni, ruled by Cunobelinus, north of the Thames, and the Atrebates to the south. On the death of Cunobelinus, a power struggle erupted between his three sons, one of whom fled to Rome for support. Verica, king of the Atrebates, also fled to Rome in AD 42 to plead for help against tribal rivals. A bungled invasion ordered by the Roman emperor Caligula had already failed, but in AD 43 the new emperor Claudius dispatched a huge invasion fleet across the English Channel.

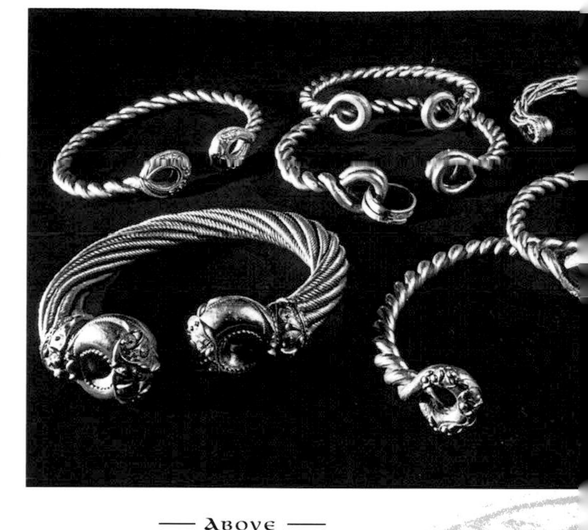

— Above —

Gold torcs from the hoards buried at Snettisham, Norfolk, 2,000 years ago display the wealth, skill and artistry of British Celts. Torcs were worn as symbols rather than accessories, and so fascinated the Romans in Britain that they awarded them to soldiers for bravery.

— Above —

The White Horse of Uffington was scoured from the chalky Berkshire downs thousands of years ago. The nearby hill fort of Uffington Castle was constructed in the 6th or 5th century BC, but the horse may be even older.

— Above —

Gold coin of Cunobelinus, bearing the Celtic leader's name and probably struck at his capital, later named Colchester.

— Right —

This horned bronze helmet dredged from the River Thames, dating around the 1st century BC, was probably ceremonial. Battle helmets, when worn, were more often made of leather, although some were decorated and bore animal crests, often a bird or boar.

Against the Romans

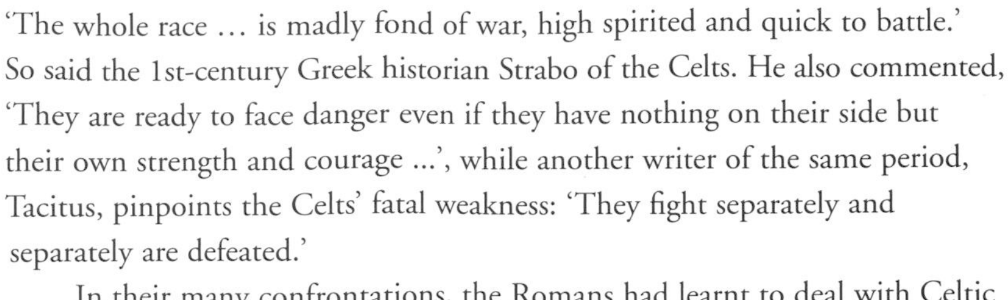

'The whole race … is madly fond of war, high spirited and quick to battle.' So said the 1st-century Greek historian Strabo of the Celts. He also commented, 'They are ready to face danger even if they have nothing on their side but their own strength and courage ...', while another writer of the same period, Tacitus, pinpoints the Celts' fatal weakness: 'They fight separately and separately are defeated.'

In their many confrontations, the Romans had learnt to deal with Celtic battle strategy. First came the terrifying din and display – screaming war cries, clashing swords on shields, blasting horns and trumpets. With their hair streaming, the Celts charged, often naked but for sword belt and gold neck torc. For centuries, however, Celts had also fought among themselves, tribe against tribe, champion against champion, competing for glory. Their armies lacked unity. A failed attack, or sustained pressure, caused loss of confidence and then panic. The Roman army, tightly ranked and disciplined, bludgeoned its remorseless way to victory.

— Below —

A Celtic warrior figure from Italy, clad only in torc, weapon belt and crested helmet. The shield is lost, as is the weapon he prepares to thrust.

— Above —

War trumpet, or carnyx, flourished aloft by a horseman on this gold coin of the Catuvellauni tribe. War horns added to the pre-battle clamour worked up by Celtic armies to scare the enemy.

— Above —

This Celtic dagger and sheath, found in the Thames at Cookham, Berkshire, was possibly a votive offering.

— Above —

The Roman army using boats to cross the Danube, under the protection of Neptune below. This panel from Trajan's Column in Rome shows well-provisioned, armed and disciplined troops. The crossing to invade Britain required equally detailed logistical planning.

Caesar's ships carried 10,000 men to Britain in 55 BC, where after an initial quick victory his fleet was damaged by storms and he withdrew. When he returned the next year, the Britons tried fighting under a single leader, the chief of the Catuvellauni. 'Scorched-earth' tactics backed up by lightning chariot attacks might have forced a Roman retreat, but tribal treachery intervened. The Trinovantes concluded a separate peace with Caesar, who took hostages, imposed taxes, and sailed away.

Power was consolidating in the south east. The Trinovantes, Rome's allies, came under the rule of Cunobelinus, chief of the Catuvellauni. When his son, Caractacus, seized land from another of Rome's allies, the new Roman emperor Claudius responded in AD 43 with an invasion by 40,000 troops. He needed stability in Britain for trade, and to strengthen his position at home.

Caractacus, with his brother Togodumnus, held up the Roman advance in a two-day battle at the River Medway. Togodumnus was killed but Caractacus escaped west, and in Wales continued as tribal resistance leader for eight more years. Betrayed finally in AD 52 by Cartimandua, queen of the northern Brigantes, he was sent to Rome but spared. He is said to have pleaded, 'If you would rule the world, does it follow that the world must welcome servitude?'

An iron sword symbolized the warrior to whom it was dedicated. Imbued with the smith's magic, personalized decoration added protective charm in battle. Celts generally wore swords on the right, sheathed in iron, bronze, wood or leather scabbards. The heavy, slashing weapon needed room to swing, while the short, stabbing Roman sword was effective in close formation. This spectacular 3rd-century BC sword from Kirkburn, Yorkshire, was enamelled in scarlet and crafted from over 70 parts. It was buried with a warrior, together with a joint of meat.

— Above —

The magnificent 'Battersea' shield of the 2nd century BC, ritually deposited in the River Thames. Bronze, inlaid with red glass, its central circular boss is typical of late La Tène British workmanship. The shield may have been made for display, or specifically as an offering.

Celtic Queen

— Above —

The boar, a potent Celtic image, might be worn as a helmet crest to signify status or as a protective symbol. This little bronze from around the 1st century BC *was found at Hounslow, Middlesex.*

British Celts were swiftly Romanized, at least superficially, as chiefs and princes exchanged thatched huts and tribal feasts for open-plan houses with bathrooms. Roman rule was at first military. As the legions advanced, they built forts linked by roads and soon had the south of the province under central control. Two tribes were granted client-kingdom status: the Atrebates of Cogidubnus, and the Iceni of Norfolk under Prasutagus.

Wales, however, remained defiant and in AD 61 Suetonius Paulinus, Britain's governor, set out to crush the Druid sanctuary of Anglesey and, with it, Celtic resistance. 'On the shore stood the enemy. Between the ranks dashed women in black, like the Furies, with their hair let down and streaming and brandishing flaming torches. Around the enemy host were Druids, uttering prayers and curses.' Apparently appalled, Paulinus proceeded to destroy the spiritual heart of Celtic Britain – just as news came that Roman Britain, too, was in flames.

On the death of Prasutagus, heavy-handed Roman officials lost no time in terminating their client-rule agreement with the East Anglian tribe. Moving in to take over, they were challenged by the king's widow, Boudicca, whereupon she was flogged and her two daughters brutally raped. The Iceni erupted in fury. Together with the Trinovantes, whose lands had been annexed for the settlement of Roman veterans around Camulodunum, the Britons stormed and burnt this new Roman capital. They were led by the Iceni warrior queen (who to Roman eyes was 'very tall ... her voice was harsh ... a great mass of red hair fell to her hips ...'). The rampaging force then fell on London (Londinium) and St Albans (Verulamium) in an orgy of slaughter.

Paulinus marched to meet them, gathering more men as he went, although the II Augusta legion failed to arrive and for that its commander was obliged to commit suicide.

— Below —

Embodiment of British resistance in AD *61, Boudicca rouses the Iceni from her bronze chariot. This 19th-century sculpture on the Victoria Embankment, London, is by Thomas Thorneycroft.*

The outcome was decided somewhere in the Midlands. As many times before, a huge Celtic force proved its own undoing. Baggage wagons at the rear of the battle line, from which women and children watched the slaughter, cut off escape from a relentless Roman thrust. The Britons were butchered. Around 80,000 died, having killed 70,000 of their enemies in the uprising. But Boudicca, choosing poison before capture, had halted Roman military expansion for a decade.

— Above —
Remains of a home at the fortified Celtic village of Din Lligwy on Anglesey, stronghold of the Druids. The Romans almost totally destroyed the Celtic religious base on the island.

— Above —
Cache of Iceni coins found in Cambridgeshire, probably hidden during Boudicca's uprising.

— Right —
The Celtic warrior on the Flannery brooch is protected by his sword (the blade is lost), helmet and shield, but is otherwise naked. The brooch probably dates from the 3rd century BC.

Celtic Legacy

— Above —

Decorated with the centuries-old patterns of Celtic swirls and spirals, this copper-gilt Irish crucifixion plaque dates from the 8th century AD and may have been part of a book cover, shrine or cross.

Celtic culture survived where Romans feared to tread – in Ireland – or where their footfall was fleeting – in Scotland and the wilds of the west. Elsewhere in Britain, it clung on to resurface after the Roman exodus around AD 410, which was hastened by Celtic attacks of Picts and Scots, together with raiding Saxons.

Without Roman troops, Britain's coastal defences could not keep out Germanic raiders from across the North Sea, or Celts from Ireland and Scotland. In the confusion of the times, a variety of British, Celtic-speaking kingdoms grew up, including Strathclyde, Gododdin and Elmet, as Saxon settlement spread in the east. When the west, too, was attacked by Saxons, the leader credited with British resistance was a hero – later known as Arthur – in the ancient Celtic mould.

During these 'Dark Ages', Celtic culture was kept alive in the Christian monasteries of Wales, Ireland and the north by missionaries in the tradition of St Patrick, a Romano-Briton kidnapped by Irish raiders. By AD 800, the Celtic world had developed a renowned literate, artistic civilization that was once more at the mercy of Germanic raiders – the Vikings. The fusion of Celtic, Saxon and Roman traditions produced such glorious illuminated manuscripts as the Book of Kells and the Lindisfarne Gospels, with interlaced geometric patterns echoing those of the ancient La Tène craftsmen.

— Right —

Glowing full-page portrait of St Matthew from the Book of Kells, a Latin gospel-book of the late 8th/early 9th century produced by monks in the Celtic tradition. Its profuse decoration of abstract geometric patterns and animal and bird ornament derives from the La Tène style. The monastery at Kells was established early in the 9th century as new headquarters for monks from Iona, founded by St Columba off the Scottish west coast.

— Left —
A relic of the Celtic St Columba may have rested in this portable 'house'-shaped shrine, the Monymusk Reliquary. This wooden box, ornamented with gilt and silver in Pictish/Irish style, was made in the late 7th or early 8th century AD, perhaps in Scotland.

Celtic kingdoms gradually came under English sway, but Celtic history and myth lived independently in the ancient language. In the 5th century, Celtic speech was returned to what had been Gaul when British colonists settled in the part of France now known as Brittany, taking the language that became Breton. The independent British had referred to themselves as 'Cymry' – fellow countrymen – a name later restricted to those in Cymru, Wales.

In the story cycles of Wales – particularly the *Mabinogion* – and of Ireland, remains of ancient Celtic mythology and history survive. So does a form of the bardic tradition in the Welsh eisteddfod. Such traditions have been exported round the world with Celtic migrants from the British Isles, so that there is a Welsh-speaking area today in Patagonia, for example.

Most modern Europeans have Celts among their ancestors, but only in Britain and Ireland have Celtic peoples survived within a culture that stretches back to the dawn of European history.

— Above —
Portrait from the Life and Miracles of St Cuthbert *(630–687) written by the Saxon historian, Bede.*

— Above —
This 5th-century stone bears characteristic decorative patterns employed by Celts since the early Iron Age.

Places to Visit

Butser Ancient Farm
near Petersfield, Hampshire
Reconstructed Celtic farm-stead

Chysauster
Cornwall
Iron-Age house remains

Danebury
near Stockbridge, Hampshire
Iron-Age hill fort

Fishbourne Roman Palace
near Chichester, East Sussex
Possible palace of Cogidubnus

Glastonbury
Somerset
Lake villages

Iceni Village and Museum
Swaffham, Norfolk
Reconstructed settlement

Iona Abbey
Iona, off Mull
Shrine of St Columba

Lindisfarne (Holy Island)
off Northumberland coast
Site of Columba's monastery

Maiden Castle
near Dorchester, Dorset
Iron-Age hill fort

Mousa Broch
Shetland
1st-century BC defensive stone tower

Old Sarum
near Salisbury, Wiltshire
Iron-Age hill fort

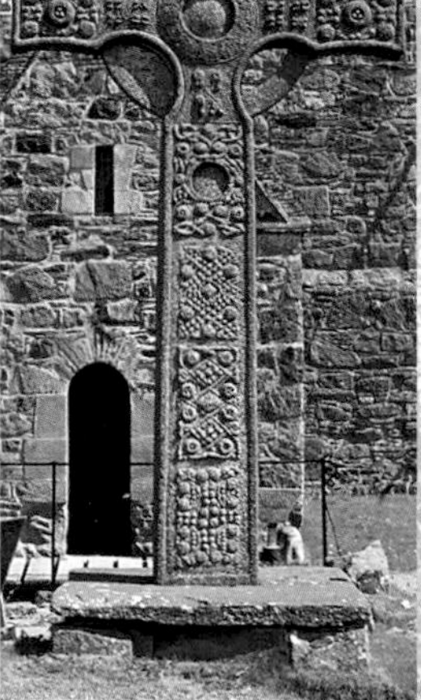

St Albans
Hertfordshire
Romano-British remains (Verulamium)

Scottish Crannog Centre
Kenmore, Tayside
Reconstructed crannog

Silchester
near Basingstoke, Hampshire
Oppidum site under Roman walls

Stanwick
Northamptonshire
Brigantian site, earthwork defences

Tara
Co. Meath
Royal site

Trinity College
Dublin
Book of Kells, Book of Durrow

MUSEUMS

British Museum
London
Celtic metalwork, Lindow Man

Colchester Castle Museum
Colchester, Essex
Iron-Age finds, Roman city remains, traces of Boudiccan revolt

Hull Museum
Kingston upon Hull, Humberside
Reconstructed chariot burials

Liverpool Museum
Liverpool, Mersey
La Tène artwork

Museum of the Iron Age
Andover, Hampshire
Finds from Danebury hill fort